Summary

We need to approach ⸻ ᴄeltic
saints with less of a c⸻ …nether events in this or
that saint's life are historically accurate or verifiable, but
rather, as earlier generations did, with an openness to what
the stories themselves might teach us about God, holiness,
and our own great mysteries.

Edward C. Sellner is professor of pastoral theology and
spirituality at the College of St. Catherine, St. Paul, Minnesota
and the author of (among other books) *Wisdom of the Celtic
Saints*, the original edition of which is familiar to many. He has
recently revised and expanded this book and published it
himself in a handsome hardback edition. Because this is now a
much more expensive book, the author has very kindly
consented to allow the Northumbria Community to publish
his excellent Introduction to the revised edition (very slightly
amended because the saints' stories themselves are not to be
found herein) as a stand-alone booklet in this 'How then shall
we live?' series.

There are many strands woven together in the cloth that forms
the ethos of the Northumbria Community. Celtic spirituality is
only one of them. However, it is perhaps the most important,
given the Community's geographical roots close to Holy
Island (where the stories of Aidan and Cuthbert and many
other Celtic saints are all-pervading), and the influence of
those saints' lives on the Community's search for answers to
the key question of 'How then shall we live?'

What follows in the booklet is a masterly introduction to the
stories of these lives as they have been handed down to us;

and to the way we should best approach them. The author puts them in the context of the origins of Celtic monasticism, the early Celtic church and Celtic spirituality. Then he provides us with some vital keys for relating to the stories we read:

- The portrayal of the saints' lives as a living symbol or image of Christ

- The significance of symbols and sacred numbers

- The importance of 'listening with our heart'

If you wish to read the detailed lives of the saints themselves, you will need to read the book itself (see detailed bibliographical information on this and other books by Ed Sellner in the Resources section at the back). *Wisdom of the Celtic Saints: Revised and Expanded Edition,* which is available by mail order from Cloisters, presents the stories of 27 of the most important Celtic saints from Ireland, Scotland, northern England, Wales, Cornwall and Brittany; and it includes good maps.

What we especially need to bring to these stories and sayings is a compassionate, attentive, listening heart.

The Founders of Celtic Monasticism

Sometimes a place holds memories that predate our own personal experiences or recollections. On the banks of the Shannon River in the heart of Ireland stand the ruins of an ancient Celtic monastery that was once one of Ireland's largest, a place of learning and of pilgrimage. Though few trees grow there now, grass colours the site with many shades of green, and, like another monastery, St. Kevin's at Glendalough, with which it was closely associated, it has its share of crosses marking numerous graves. Two large round towers still stand that were once used as bell-towers to call the monks to prayer and possibly as look-out points to warn them of hostile enemies. Down the road from what was once the men's monastic buildings lie the ruins of the Nuns' Church where centuries ago religious women gathered throughout the day and night to pray. Within the new Visitor Centre that was constructed in the early 1990s the four high crosses, beautifully carved out of stone, which once graced the monastic site are now protected from the elements. Though the bright colours of their original paint have long since faded, darkened by the weather and the passage of time, the images on the crosses still tell the story of Jesus and the lives of the Celtic saints.

Ciaran's search for wisdom

The most stunning of these crosses is called 'the Cross of the Scriptures' because of its depiction of the crucifixion on one side and Christ in his glory on the other. It also shows scenes of a king of Ireland helping the founder of the monastery build the first church, and of reconciliation between two hostile Irish kings, possibly brought about through the ministry of a later abbot.

This is the home of St. Ciaran, one of the earliest founders of Celtic monasticism. The monastery he founded in 545 is Clonmacnois, next to Armagh, the most prominent home of religion and culture in the Early Irish Church. Here missionaries were trained who would take the Christian faith to Britain and continental Europe; here men and women, numbering as many as a thousand, perhaps more, prayed for and ministered to each other for over a thousand years.

An early story in the *Book of Lismore,* a medieval manuscript, tells of this Ciaran, the son of a chariot-maker, who at an early age leaves his parents in order to learn wisdom. His search for wisdom becomes a life-long trait, and the wisdom he acquires seems to come as a result of his deep friendship with certain spiritual mentors. From his teacher Finnian of Clonard, Ciaran learns the art of healing and the importance of teaching wisdom to others, beginning with the young daughter of an Irish king; from his spiritual guide Enda, he is given the courage to pursue his vocation and to found a church at Clonmacnois; and, from his close friend Kevin of Glendalough, he receives communion and a final blessing at the time of his early death at 33.

While each of the stories of Ciaran gives us intimations about how wisdom is acquired as well as the importance of spiritual mentors in our lives, the one of Ciaran's visit to Enda stands out in its unexpectedly vivid imagery. We are told that at the time Ciaran arrived on Inis Mor, one of the Aran Islands in Galway Bay, where Enda was living, both men beheld the same vision of a great tree growing in the middle of Ireland. This tree, while protecting Ireland, also had its fruit carried across the Irish Sea by birds from around the world which filled its branches. Struck by the vision's force, Ciaran turned to Enda and told him what he had seen. Enda, in turn, interpreted for him the symbolic language of the vision, telling him that the great tree which they saw 'is you, Ciaran, for you are great in the eyes of God.' He continued: 'All of Ireland will be sheltered by the grace within you, and many people will be fed by your fasting and prayers. So, go in the name of God to the centre of the island, and found your church on the banks of a stream.'

Self-awareness, self-acceptance, wholeness and holiness

Anyone who knows Ciaran's story and visits the early Christian site of Clonmacnois can almost feel the powerful presence and holiness of this Celtic saint who, according to that early writing, became recognized as a charismatic leader, gifted teacher, and compassionate soulfriend. To walk the winding paths among the ruins, and to stand on the same bank of the Shannon where he once stood is to encounter first-hand the wisdom of those early Celtic saints, a wisdom rooted in their spirituality.

This booklet is about the wisdom of the Celtic saints, those inspired pioneers of the Early Celtic Church who helped the Christian faith take root and flourish in Ireland, Britain, and on the continent of Europe itself. Like Ciaran, many of them were founders of monasteries which became religious, cultural, and educational centres for leaders, both clerical and lay, during the early Middle Ages. Others travelled as missionaries and pilgrims throughout the world, bringing Christianity not only to the European continent, but possibly to North America as well – centuries before Columbus. All of them were teachers, confessors, and soulfriends to countless numbers of people.

One of the main sources that sheds light on Celtic spirituality and soulfriendship are the stories and sayings which appear in the *acta sanctorum* or Lives of the Saints. These Lives of the Celtic saints were primarily compiled in the high medieval period (13-16th centuries), but many were written in the sixth through ninth centuries. Almost all have primitive material that take us back to the earliest days of the Celtic Church. As such, they are part of the history of Christian hagiography, a particular genre of literature written to present the saints as worthy spiritual mentors who can inspire us, and whose admirable qualities we might integrate into our own personalities and lives. Though not historically accurate biographies as we understand that term today, they do express the larger truths of the saints' lives that moved them (and can move us) toward greater self-awareness and self-acceptance, wholeness and holiness, meaning and God.

In order for the reader to more fully understand and appreciate the stories and sayings of the early Celtic saints which have become available to us today, it is helpful briefly to consider the history of the Early Celtic Church and specific characteristics of its spirituality as well as examine the religious pattern that underlies many of the stories and the symbolic language which they contain. Finally, a specific approach to reading them will be discussed. All of this, I hope, will better prepare the reader for grasping and beginning to integrate Celtic wisdom in our own time.

The Early Celtic Church

Long before the theological and political conflicts tragically divided Christianity, one of its most ancient and creative churches grew to prominence. This Celtic Church existed from the 5th to the 12th centuries, and during its time kept classical learning alive while the so-called 'Dark Ages' were casting their shadows across Europe. It was made up of a great variety of churches in such places as Northern England, Cornwall, Wales, Scotland, the Isle of Man, Brittany in France, Galicia in Spain, and, of course, all of Ireland. Although these churches were never linked through administrative structures nor dependent upon a hierarchical 'chain of command', theirs was a spiritual community united through a communion of friendships and alliances between spiritual leaders and their monasteries. Numerous stories in the hagiographies which portray the monastic founders studying, working, travelling together, and frequently mentoring each other reflect how their hagiographers desired to show that these churches were, in fact, spiritually connected.

These Celtic churches were not cut off from the more Romanized churches on the Continent nor the bishop of Rome – although certain Irish leaders, St. Columban (c. 543-615) in particular, were not adverse to arguing directly with the Pope. They did, however, have a preference for the monastic and hermit life. 'The history of the Celtic Church,' says Welsh scholar G.H. Doble, 'is largely a history of monks and monasteries.' Although there was certainly much diversity in this Early Celtic Church if one considers the different countries in which it grew and the differences that developed over the centuries, it maintained **A preference for** its identity and fundamental unity **the monastic** through its storytelling, music, art, **and hermit life** liturgical and private prayers, all of which were expressions of its spirituality, a spirituality which was highly corporate in nature, emphasizing, as it did, the spiritual bonds of tribe, family, and soulfriends.

This Celtic Christian spirituality was very much the child of the ancient pagan culture which preceded it, one that valued poetic imagination and artistic creativity, kinship relations and the warmth of a hearth, the wonder of stories and the guidance of dreams. It was a spirituality profoundly affected by the beauty of the landscape, the powerful presence of the sea, and the swift passage at night of the full moon across open skies. Baptized in the waters of Christian faith by such leaders as Patrick, Brigit, and Columcille (Ireland's 'holy trinity' of saints) this pagan spirituality eventually flowered into monastic cities, high crosses, illuminated gospels, and a ministry of spiritual mentoring that changed profoundly the course of Christian spirituality.

No one knows precisely when the Christian faith arrived in Ireland and the British Isles, but there are a number of fascinating legends about the spread of Christianity to that part of the world. Some say that either Sts. Peter or Paul travelled to Britain and established the church there; others tell how Joseph of Arimathea, who had cared for the body of Christ, came to Glastonbury and planted a thorn from Christ's head near a small church in sight of the famous Tor. Besides these legends, there are the stories about the Celtic saints themselves who lived, worked, and prayed in Ireland and throughout Britain. Although details about the earliest of them are historically vague, these latter tales bring us closer to the geographical and spiritual landscape of the Early Celtic Church. Ninian is said to have founded a monastery, *Candida Casa* (the 'White House'), at Whithorn in southern Scotland in 397 which became an important place for educating missionaries and laity. Patrick is credited with bringing the Christian faith to Ireland in 432, but there were Christians living on that island years before his arrival. In 596, Augustine, the first archbishop of Canterbury, was sent by Pope Gregory the Great (c. 540-604) to evangelize the people in southern England, while northern England came under the influence of missionaries from Iona. Between the fifth and eighth centuries Wales and Brittany were christianized by wandering monks and missionaries, many of them from Ireland.

The sixth century especially saw the rise of the great monasteries in Ireland and the Celtic parts of Britain. These monasteries were headed by powerful abbesses or abbots, such as Brigit of Kildare, Columcille (Columba) of Iona, Finnian of Clonard, Ita of Killeedy, Brendan of Clonfert, Kevin of Glendalough, Ciaran of Clonmacnois, and David of Wales. Many of the first male founders and abbots of these monasteries, as the early hagiographies maintain, were probably celibate priests and bishops. Women founders and abbesses also lived celibate lives within religious communities. This way of life was chosen because of the value the early church placed on virginity, in imitation of Christ, and because, for women in particular, the monastic life offered the opportunity to develop one's intellectual abilities and creative pursuits. It was the only alternative to the roles of wife and mother in marriage, or, in spinsterhood, that of maintaining a household for aging parents and unmarried siblings. In the case of the male monastic leaders who followed the early pioneers, these men might have been either ordained or lay. Many were evidently married, since the marriage of priests throughout the entire early church was commonplace and the Celtic Church was no exception. In some Irish monasteries, in fact, the abbacy descended from father to son.

Simplicity of life and equality of all in the sight of God

By the seventh century a distinct form of Christianity had emerged in Ireland and Britain. Within the universal church from its earliest days there already was much diversity: differences rooted in racial, cultural, and historical developments which affected the leadership of the local churches and their understanding of Christianity. The Early Celtic Church, however, was especially unique. Influenced greatly by the values of the ancient Celtic culture which preceded the arrival of Christianity on its shores, as well as the ideals of the early desert Christians who valued simplicity of life and the equality of all in the eyes of God, this Celtic Church frequently found itself in conflict with other churches, including the church in Rome, over issues specifically related to church governance and sexuality.

Many of the other Western churches, adopting the social structures of the declining Roman Empire as their own, divided church territory into dioceses, headed by bishops who lived primarily in urban areas. The Early Celtic Church, however, was located more often in rural or remote areas and influenced by the tribal system of the ancient Celts. Monastic leaders who emerged at the great Celtic monasteries were eventually more powerful than the bishops who lived in their midst. Even when leadership was limited to celibates or the ordained, the monasteries themselves had many lay people (known as *manaigh*) attached to them. Both celibate members within the monastic communities as well as these lay people experienced the fruits of collaboration: education, pastoral care, and liturgical leadership were provided by the monks or religious women; in turn, lay people and their families helped the monasteries grow their crops, manage their farms, fish, plant trees, and keep their bees. All benefited from this mutual sharing of gifts, including those who only came for a short stay. As one of the earliest hagiographers, Cogitosus, writes about those who came to the monastery of St. Brigit at Kildare: 'Who can list the chaotic crowds and countless folk who flock in from all the provinces: some for the abundance of food, others who are feeble seeking health, others just to look at the mobs, and still others who come with great gifts to the festival of Saint Brigit.'

Differences between Roman-style and Celtic churches also emerged over time as the Roman Empire was broken apart by invading Germanic tribes, including the Anglo-Saxons who swept into Britain in the 5th century, driving many Celts into those geographical areas now identified as Scotland, Wales, Cornwall, and Brittany. While the other ecclesial bodies came to value large churches and basilicas for their communal liturgies, the Celtic Church built small ones of wood and, later, stone. Even when the membership in the monasteries increased, the Celtic Christians, wanting to maintain greater intimacy among their members, continued to build more numerous and smaller church dwellings rather than larger structures for worship. Also, as the continental churches grew increasingly more materialistic, dressing their bishops in fine vestments and having them ride on golden thrones (as described in the *Life of Wilfrid*, a Northumbrian saint), the Celtic Church valued a more ascetic lifestyle.

Inspired by the life-stories of the desert father St. Antony (251-356) and of the anchorite bishop of Tours, St. Martin (c. 316-397), the Celtic churches were characterized by intense missionary outreach, a pastoral ministry among the common people, and leaders who ate sparsely and spent long hours in prayer, sometimes immersed nightly in the ocean's frigid waters. The early Celtic monastic bishops themselves, such as David of Wales and Aidan of Lindisfarne, dressed simply, clad in coarse robes, usually carrying with them on their pastoral visits only a walking stick and a bell which, as they approached, would be loudly rung to alert the local people. (Celestine, bishop of Rome in the early fifth century did not appreciate what he called their 'innovation' in dress. He condemned in a letter, *Cuperemus quidem*, the appointment of Celtic 'wanderers and strangers' over the

Intense missionary outreach; pastoral ministry among the common people

local clergy in Gaul who 'clad in a cloak, and with a girdle round the loins' are 'changing the usage of so many years, of such great prelates, for another [type of] habit.')

Again, differences between the churches related to sexuality arose. While the other Christian churches increasingly isolated women from positions of authority and relationships of friendship with males, the Celtic Church, influenced by the ancient Celts' belief that women were equal to men and had similar legal rights, encouraged their leadership. Contrary to the prevailing dualistic tendencies found among desert Christians and the inhabitants of countries bordering the Mediterranean, the early founders of the Celtic Church 'did not reject,' according to a 9th-century manuscript, *Catalogue of the Saints in Ireland*, 'the service and society of women.' Women were valued and not ignored, judging from one of the earliest Irish martyrologies, that of Gorman, which lists over two hundred female saints. Monastic communities which arose in Ireland shortly after the death of Patrick in 461 were also headed by women. The oldest monasteries of women recorded in Ireland are those of Brigit of Kildare, Moninne at Killeavy, and Ita at Killeedy.

Many of these women leaders held powerful ecclesial positions in communities consisting of both women and men. These 'double monasteries' were evidently a normal feature

Women were valued and their leadership encouraged

of the earliest monastic life in Ireland and England. The most well-known abbesses over these double monasteries were Brigit, who founded a community at Kildare, Ireland, and Hild of Whitby, Northumbria. (Hild, of Anglo-Saxon origins, received her religious formation from Aidan of Lindisfarne and was very much affected by and in sympathy with the Celtic monks and their spirituality.) The origins of these double monasteries of monks and nuns is unclear although Cogitosus, the seventh-century hagiographer of Brigit, describes the one at Kildare as a double monastery that must have originated at least one hundred years before he wrote. There the monks and nuns lived in separate quarters, but worshipped together in a common church in which the lay people joined them for liturgies. In England, during the seventh century, double monasteries were quite numerous, for we know of such establishments at Coldingham, Ely, Repton, Barking, Bardney, Wimborne, and Wenlock. This feature of the Celtic and Anglo-Saxon churches the Roman-appointed Theodore of Tarsus did not initially approve, but accepted as the custom of the land when he arrived at Canterbury in 669 to become archbishop – after a plague had wiped out most of the English episcopate. What is clear from early biographies of Brigit, as well as the stories of Hild is that such powerful abbesses exercised an influence on their times that has almost no parallel in later history – except perhaps for Hildegard of Bingen in the 12th century and Teresa of Avila in the 16th. Unfortunately, most of those double monasteries were destroyed by the Vikings in the 9th century when they laid waste to so much of the Celtic Church's monasteries and artistic treasures.

Another area related to sexuality in the Early Celtic Church that met with vehement condemnations from church authorities on the Continent had to do with the Celtic missionaries close ministerial association with women. Judging from protests against the practice, these missionaries evidently travelled quite frequently with women companions, some of whom helped with the celebration of the Eucharist. According to a sixth-century letter written by bishops in Brittany to Irish missionaries:

> Through a report made by the venerable Sparatus, we have learned that you continually carry around from one of your fellow-countrymen's huts to another, certain tables upon which you celebrate the divine sacrifice of the Mass, assisted by women whom you call *conhospitae;* and while you distribute the eucharist, they take the chalice and administer the blood of Christ to the people. This is an innovation, an unheard-of superstition ... For the love of Christ, and in the name of

the Church United and of our common faith, we beg you to renounce immediately upon receipt of this letter, these abuses of the table ... We appeal to your charity, not only to restrain these little women from staining the holy sacraments by administering them illicitly, but also not to admit to live under your roof any woman who is not your grandmother, your mother, your sister or your niece.

Although tensions between the two forms of Christianity eventually led to open disagreements at the Synod of Whitby in 664 over such issues as when Easter should be celebrated and what form of tonsure or hairstyle should be worn by the ordained, these other differences, intimately related to each other's concept of church, ministerial leadership, and spirituality, were far more important. They ultimately resulted in the submersion of the Celtic Church in Ireland by the Roman ecclesial system in the 12th century.

Survival of Celtic Christian spirituality despite supremacy of the Roman system

Still, despite that 'reform,' which was a triumph for administrators but a tragedy for Irish culture and creativity, Celtic Christian spirituality survived in various geographical locations where the saints had once lived or journeyed. It deeply affected directly or indirectly certain religious traditions and wisdom figures, including Hildegard of

Bingen, Francis of Assisi, Julian of Norwich, Joan of Arc, George Herbert, Evelyn Underhill, and Thomas Merton. In many ways, this Celtic spirituality is the foundation of Anglican, Episcopalian, and Methodist spirituality, and, because of its love of the desert fathers and mothers, it has a great affinity with that of the Eastern Orthodox. With its focus upon nature and the entire spiritual realm, and its respect for ancestors, visions, and dreams, it finds resonance with Native American and African spiritualities too. Thus, the spirituality of the Christian Celts has great ecumenical value, for it transcends the differences of the Church in the West and East which have divided Christians since before the Reformation. It also has special appeal for many of us today who are concerned about the ecological survival of our planet, the revitalization of our churches, and the quality of our own spiritual life.

This Celtic Christian spirituality is especially reflected in the hagiographies of the saints. Within their stories and sayings we will be able to discern key characteristics of that spirituality which we may want to integrate into our own lives, work, and ministries.

A sense of wonder and awe at the divine residing in everything

Celtic Spirituality

One of the primary characteristics of the early Celtic Christians was their love of and respect for the physical environment. Their daily life was lived in close proximity to nature, and their spirituality reflected what the Welsh call *hud*: a sense of wonder and awe at the divine residing in everything. Their pagan ancestors, like other indigenous peoples, had a deep respect for nature, regarding the earth as a mother, the source of all fertility. Their spiritual leaders, the druids and druidesses, believed that the supernatural pervaded every aspect of life, and that spirits were everywhere: in ancient trees and sacred groves, mountaintops and rock formations, rivers, streams, and holy wells. Influenced by that ancient spiritual heritage, Celtic Christians found it natural to address God as 'Lord of the Elements', and to experience communion with God in their natural surroundings. In the stories of the saints, they are often found establishing their monasteries and oratories in places where the druids and druidesses had once taught and worshipped: in the midst of oak groves or near sacred springs, on the shores of secluded lakes, or on misty islands far out at sea. This attitude of deep respect for the environment was also manifest in their quiet care for all living things. The Celtic saints seem to have had a special affinity with animals in relationships that were reciprocated: Kevin shelters in his hands a blackbird which probably sang for him, Ciaran meets a wild boar who helps him clear land for his monastery, Columcille's white horse sheds great tears at his master's approaching death. Animals are portrayed as fellow creatures of the earth, and, once befriended, they become helpers to the saints.

A second characteristic of these Christian Celts, inherited from their druidic mentors, was their love of learning. Christian Ireland in particular was the place where monastic schools flourished, and where the original pagan Celtic legends and stories of the saints were first written down in the monastic scriptoria. According to the great storyteller, Bede the Venerable (c. 672-735), many pilgrim scholars came to Ireland from Britain and the continent of Europe to study and learn:

> In the course of time some of these devoted themselves faithfully to the monastic life, while others preferred to travel round to the cells of various teachers and apply themselves to study. The Irish welcomed them all gladly, gave them their daily food, and also provided them with books to read and with instruction, without asking for any payment.

Inspired, surely, by the teachers and tutors they encountered living in those cells, the

Respect for study and yearning for wisdom

visitors must have learned a great deal about holiness and God. We can see this respect for study and yearning for wisdom in the frequent references to books in the hagiographies of the early Celtic saints. We also find those characteristics in specific stories; for example, in Aidan's encouraging all those who travelled with him to study sometime each day, and in Columcille's spending so much time alone in his cell to study and write. Irish missionaries, like Columban, brought this love of learning to France, Switzerland, Germany, and Italy where they founded other great monastic schools which kept Celtic wisdom alive for generations after the deaths of the original saintly pioneers.

A third characteristic associated with the early Christian Celts and revealed in the stories of the saints is their innate yearning to explore the unknown. Perhaps this *wanderlust* was due to the migratory nature of their ancient ancestors who in the 3rd century B.C. had been the dominant race of all of Europe; perhaps it was their living in such close proximity to the sea and the natural rhythm of its tides; perhaps their Judeo-Christian spiritual heritage unconsciously inspired them with its own stories of Jonah in the belly of the whale, of Abraham and Sarah's travel to a foreign land, of Moses' exodus out of Egypt, and of Peter and Paul's missionary journeys.

Whatever the reason, many of them shared the desire to travel, crossing not only the European continent, but even reaching Kiev in Russia by the 9th century. In contrast to the 'red martyrdom' of giving one's life up for Christ or the 'green martyrdom' of participating in severe penitential practices, they faced the 'white martyrdom' of living years far from home and hearth for the sake of the gospels. (The Celts had a specific word, *hiraeth*, for the extreme yearning for home associated with this latter form of martyrdom; because of their deep love of tribe and family, it was considered the hardest of all to endure.) Beginning with St. Patrick, Celtic missionaries (called *peregrini*) chose this way of life out of deep devotion to Christ, but also perhaps because of their genuine appreciation of God's mysterious creation and their own desire to see the holy places and meet people different than themselves.

Whatever the reasons for their travel, this theme of pilgrimage is one of the key elements of the early saints' spirituality. For them, to make a 'Journey for Christ' brought – despite the hardships – unexpected blessings, increased intimacy with God, and the healing of body and soul. Brendan the Navigator is, of course, the most famous of these pilgrims, but there are others as well. Each saint is profoundly affected by his or her journeys, and returns with new experiences and wisdom to share with those who remained at home. A chain of mentoring is formed, and the monasteries which the early saints founded and the tombs where their bodies are placed for the Day of Resurrection become, in turn, important sites to which others journey on pilgrimage.

A fourth characteristic of Celtic spirituality is the Celtic Christians' love of silence and of solitude. Considering the widespread travel of so many *peregrini* and the extensive pastoral work of all the Celtic saints, what is intriguing and somewhat paradoxical is how much the early Christian Celts also valued solitary places and times of silence. They perhaps sought out places of solitude precisely because of their intense involvement with people. An atmosphere of silence was encouraged within their monasteries and certain quiet times were strictly observed, as we find, for example, in the stories of David of Wales. Many of the Celtic monasteries also had a place apart, a cell, retreat, or *dysert* in which a monk or nun could retire when he or she needed to be alone. Sometimes the Celtic saints chose a cave for shelter and reflection, as did Columban and Ninian of Whithorn (362-432). Others moved to a hill or mountaintop to fast and pray. Many, as is clear in the stories of Aidan, Columcille, Declan, and Cuthbert, seemed especially drawn to be near the ocean's waves. Whatever their reasons for treasuring silence and seeking

White martyrdom: living for years far from home

the solitary life, the early Christian Celts shared what the scholar John Ryan calls a 'surprising' combination of 'apostolic and anchoretical ideals.'

A fifth characteristic of Celtic spirituality has to do with their understanding of time. The early saints appreciated time as a sacred reality blessed and **already** redeemed by God's overflowing compassion. This awareness of the sacred dimension to time is not the same as contemporary Western culture's frantic preoccupation with it in which 'every minute counts.' Rather, the Celts' perception was that there is a fullness **now** to all of time, manifest in the old Irish saying, 'when God made time, he made plenty of it.' With this perception of time as a gift from God, time in a chronological sense (with one historical event following another) was disregarded by the early Celts. For them, the present contains within itself both past events which continue to live on, as well as the seeds of future events waiting to be born.

When God made time, he made plenty of it

Without clear demarcations between past, present, and future, Celtic Christians interpreted history differently than we do. They made contemporaries of those who historically could never have been. In some of the early legends, for example, Brigit and Ita are portrayed as midwives to Mary, the mother of Jesus, and, as soulfriends, help bring Jesus to birth and to nurse him; or, in the certain stories about Brigit and Patrick, both are described as intimate friends – when in fact they most probably never met. (If the traditional dates of their lives are relied upon, Brigit would have only been about six years old at the time of Patrick's death.) That did not matter to the early Christian Celts, for, from their point of view, people with the qualities and holiness of Patrick and Brigit would naturally be friends – even if they lived at different times in the chronological sequence of history.

In many ways, Celtic Christians saw the larger truths of myth and the lasting effects of relationships of love standing outside of time, having an eternal quality to them that certainly cannot be fully understood by considering chronological time alone. The early Celts also believed in 'thin places': geographical locations scattered throughout Ireland and other Celtic lands where they experienced only a very thin 'divide' between past and present and future times; where a person is somehow able, possibly only for a moment, to encounter a more ancient reality within present time; or where perhaps only in a glance we are somehow transported into the future. Some of the stories which associate the saints with intuitive and psychic powers attest to these 'thin places.' Other stories of certain saints who communicate with each other after the death of one of them, such as Ciaran and Kevin, and Maedoc and Columcille, affirm the existence not only of thin places but also of bonds of soulfriendship which death itself can never destroy.

A sixth characteristic of Celtic spirituality, related to their concept of time, was the Celtic Christians' appreciation of ordinary life. Recognizing time as a reality made holy by a loving God, the Celtic saints valued the daily, the routine, the ordinary. They believed that God is found not so much at the end of time when the Reign of God **finally** comes, but **now**, where the Reign is already being lived by God's faithful people. Theirs was a spirituality characterized by gratitude, and, in their stories we find them worshipping God in their daily work and very ordinary chores. Another quality, their joy, is apparent in David of Wales' last words to his friends: 'My brothers and sisters, be joyful, keep your faith and belief, and perform the small things which you have learned from me and have seen in me.' Seeing their daily lives as revelatory of God's love, they valued the cyclical dimension of time, believing that by immersing themselves in the seasons of the year and uniting their lives with the liturgical seasons of the Church, they could more effectively celebrate time's sacredness as well as their own sacred journeys through time. This perception is especially evident in the stories of St. Brendan of Clonfert which tell how he

Valuing the daily, the routine, the ordinary

and his crew celebrated feasts, such as Easter and Christmas, in a certain way and at the same places each year. Daily routines and yearly observances, the Christian Celts believed, are not boring. Rather, they can help us realize the immanence of God in time and the inherent holiness of our lives when we immerse ourselves in God's time.

A seventh characteristic of the spirituality of Celtic Christians was their belief in the great value of kinship relationships, especially the spiritual ties of soulfriends. The ancient Celts in Ireland and throughout Europe valued their families and their tribal affiliations. A fosterage system was developed by them in which children of one family were frequently brought up by another family or tribe. They believed that such exchanges not only strengthened alliances between them, but introduced each child to a wider world of learning. The ancient Celts' druids and druidesses also acted as teachers of the tribes and advisers to the kings. Like Native American and Hmong shamans, they functioned as mediators between the tribes and the spiritual realm: the world of tribal gods, goddesses, and spirits. These types of mentoring relationships survived when Christianity arrived.

In the hagiographies, we find numerous stories about younger people being guided and educated by the Celtic saints at their monasteries or cells. As the story of Ciaran of Clonmacnois and his mentor Enda shows, each of the early saints seems to have had at least one personal mentor: a wiser, more experienced, sometimes older teacher, confessor, or spiritual guide. (Holiness, not age, however, seems to be a more important criterion of such a person.) Called an *anamchara* by the Irish and Scots, and a *periglour* or *beriglour* by the Welsh, this soulfriend was not necessarily male nor ordained. Some of the greatest and most well-known of the soulfriends in the Early Celtic Church were women, such as abbesses Ita, Brigit, Samthann, and Hild. Not only were these women teachers, administrators, guides, preachers, and confessors who, as is in the stories of St. Ita, did not hesitate to give out penances, but at least two of them, according to early hagiographies, had in their possession religious articles traditionally associated with a bishop: Brigit, in Cogitosus's Life, receives a pallium (a bishop's mantle), and, in a later hagiography, she is said to have been ordained; Samthann had a marvelous crozier (a bishop's staff) which was able to perform miracles.

Besides human soulfriends, female and male, many of the saints had angelic ones. Christian Celts believed in the existence of these invisible guides whose leader was identified as the archangel Michael or, in Patrick's case, as Victor. Manifestations of

Open and honest acknowledgement of concerns, grief and spiritual diseases

God's care, these angels seem to appear at crucial turning-points in the lives of the saints when they baptize the saints, name them, appear in their dreams, help them discern their vocations, and lead them to the sites of their monasteries and eventually to their own Places of Resurrection.

What all of the stories and sayings of the Celtic saints reveal is that mentoring and spiritual guidance were considered an important, if not essential part of Celtic Christian spirituality. All the saints seem to have been changed profoundly by these relationships – whether their mentors were human or angelic, or whether they offered a compassionate ear or a challenging word. They were keenly aware, as are many today, that inner healing happens when we openly and honestly acknowledge to another person our concerns, grief, and spiritual diseases; that God is very close to those who speak as friends do, heart to heart. While there are other characteristics of Celtic spirituality that can be found in the stories of the saints, such as their valuing dreams as sources of spiritual wisdom, and their love of storytelling, music, poetry, and dance, one of the greatest discoveries of the Christian Celts, according to scholar Nora Chadwick, is 'the range and significance of individual experience, and the interest and the humour of little things, and how exciting and valuable it is to share them with one another.' This, of course, is what many would equate with the value and joy of having a soulfriend: a person with whom we can share the significant and often insignificiant experiences of our lives and discover, often in the telling, that the seemingly insignificant events are really the most important of all, the times when and places where God speaks.

Spiritual kinship with Jesus

Anyone who reads the Lives of the Celtic saints will soon recognize that each saint is portrayed not only as an extraordinary person, but above all as an *imago Christi*, that is, as a living symbol or image of Christ. This way of identifying a saint, of course, is nothing new in the history of Christian spirituality, for from the beginning of Christian life, each of us, through baptism, is welcomed into a community and hopefully begins to integrate in a lifelong process the significant values, attributes, and perspectives associated with Jesus himself. Although many of the Celtic hagiographies were inspired by and some of the contents borrowed wholesale from other earlier writings such as Athanasius's *Life of Antony*, Cassian's *Conferences*, and Sulpicius Severus's *Life of St. Martin* (of Tours), the ultimate Christian literary source for all of them were

the gospel stories. We thus find the Celtic saints doing in their time with their contemporaries what Jesus did in his: healing the sick, feeding the hungry, praying in solitude, having intimate friendships with both women and men, calming the sea, even raising the dead. Like Jesus's story too, the future significance and shape of their lives are sometimes announced in extraordinary predictions and dreams. Like him, their ministries are filled with tension, conflict, and times of grief and despair.

Overall, when one considers the stories of the Celtic saints found in the early Lives, a pattern can be discerned which is similar to the one found in Jesus's own life and ministry. It is this pattern with the following stages that lies behind many of the stories of the Celtic saints.

The **first stage** in a saint's Life usually begins with mention of the saint's distinguished ancestry and with descriptions of how the saint's birth was preceded by extraordinary events and prophetic dreams. As in the opening chapters of the Gospels of Matthew and Luke which describe Jesus's conception and birth, Brigit's birth, for example, is foretold by a druid; Brendan's mother has a vision in which her breasts shine like snow; Columcille's mother dreams of a cloak of many colours; and Findbarr, while yet in his mother's womb, cries out to the king to spare his parents from destruction. Certain holy people are also often present shortly after the birth of the saint to confirm the newborn's future greatness – similar to the story in Luke in which the elderly Simeon and the prophetess Anna speak prophecy to Joseph and Mary when they bring Jesus as a child to the Temple (Luke 2: 22-38).

A **second stage** occurs when the saint finds a worthy mentor or mentors, human and angelic, from whom wisdom is learned. Jesus, as is shown in the Gospel of Mark, went to John the Baptist, received affirmation from the Spirit of God at his baptism, and was cared for by angels after his temptations in the wilderness. In the lives of the Celtic saints, mention has already been made of the vast networks of friendships between them, and the mentoring which they received from childhood on. In these stories, some of the most outstanding examples reflecting this second stage are the guidance Ciaran receives from Finnian and Enda, Brendan from Ita, Hild from Aidan, and Cuthbert from Boisil. The Celtic saints also consistently receive help from both angels and animals who act as their guides.

A **third stage** in the stories of the saints recounts becoming a spiritual leader or mentor for others after the saint has experienced transformation and grown in spiritual wisdom. This is found in the gospels: how Jesus, after leaving the wilderness in which he has confronted his own demons, calls his first disciples at the Sea of Galilee (Mark 1:16 ff.), and then proceeds to gather a group of both women and men around him in order to teach them what he knows. So also with the Celtic saints. Though varying in degrees of enthusiasm (Kevin of Glendalough, for one, wants to be left alone), each of the saints – sometimes early in adult life, sometimes later in maturity – eventually attracts a following, builds a monastery, and offers guidance to those who come for help.

A **fourth stage** that appears in saints' lives is their performing of miracles which demonstrate their spiritual power and intimacy with God. These worthy and miraculous deeds frequently take the form of Jesus's own, such as healing the sick, casting out demons, multiplying food, and changing water into wine. (The Celtic saints, such as Brigit, however, seem to prefer beer to wine!) All of the numerous references to miraculous deeds show that miracles are not dependent so much upon the saints' own abilities, as upon their compassion – and upon their crying out in prayer to a merciful, all-powerful God. This is the underlying theological lesson behind the stories of the saints: how important it is to unite our life with God's, and how all sorts of amazing things happen when we do.

We find the Celtic saints doing in their time what Jesus did in his

A **fifth stage** in the pattern of the saints' lives

is that of travelling to other parts of the country (as Jesus did throughout his public ministry and on his journey to Jerusalem) or to foreign shores. The Celtic saints frequently visit each other's monasteries, as we find Brigit, Canair, Columcille, and Samthann doing – sometimes to teach, to learn, or just to renew old friendships. They also travel abroad to visit Christian holy places or to bring Christianity to those who have not yet heard the Good News. Some, like Findbarr, Kevin, Maedoc, and Petroc go to Rome, while others, like Aidan, Brendan, Non, Ia, and Samson walk to distant peoples or sail to unknown shores. David of Wales, according to his hagiographer, even goes to Jerusalem where he is consecrated bishop.

A **sixth stage** that appears in many hagiographies relates that the saints seem to intuit the approach of their death. The Celtic saints consistently prepare their followers for their departure, and sometimes, despite their own fears of dying, they seem to offer those who will be left behind more comfort than they themselves receive. Many of the saints impart final words of wisdom as a sacred legacy – much as Jesus did at the Last Supper and on the cross. This intuition about approaching death is expressed in the stories when a saint is forewarned by a divine visitor or when an angel leads him or her to their true Place of Resurrection. Some of the most

Being changed profoundly by Jesus and his story

moving stories are those describing the deaths of the saints, and what they tell their followers usually before – or sometimes after – they have died.

Finally, a **seventh stage** can be perceived in the miracles and marvellous happenings which occur after the death of the beloved saint. Fire, for example, appears at Patrick's tomb; a violent storm is calmed after the death of Columcille; the sun shines for twelve days straight when Findbarr dies. These accounts are similar to those events originally associated with the death of Jesus when the veil of the Temple was torn in two, the earth quaked, rocks split, and the dead rose from their graves (Matthew 27: 51 ff.). As in the stories of Jesus's resurrection, the dead saints appear to their friends, sometimes in dreams or in visions in which their souls are seen to be carried to heaven. Cures occur at their tombs. Although unusual phenomena, Christian Celts in reading those stories did not find them at all unbelievable, since they were very much convinced that the faithful dead were truly still alive. They also knew from their own experiences that God works in mysterious ways, and that when someone dies people sometimes do know intuitively of their deaths or are healed unexpectedly at their graves; that nature itself sometimes manifests its unity with humankind by sending signs that it recognizes the passing of those who have led holy lives.

These seven stages make up a pattern that reflects each saint's spiritual kinship with Jesus. All of them, by uniting their hearts and minds with Jesus, were changed profoundly by him and his story. By implication, this pattern suggested to the readers of those hagiographies that their own spirituality was meant to be shaped, as the saints' lives were, by Jesus. This pattern can be discerned in many of the stories of the Celtic saints, though the stages do not necessarily follow precisely in the order outlined. These stages are not always apparent in the Lives of the female saints, because so many of their stories are fragmentary or incomplete, appearing in the hagiographies of male saints rather than in their own. Tragically, few of the women's monasteries were wealthy enough to be able to afford a hagiographer, while others, because of their size, were the first to be destroyed by the invading Vikings. Their stories, like so many women's stories today, need to be recovered and retold for the wisdom they contain.

Symbols and sacred numbers

Besides the religious pattern the hagiographers used to represent the saints' paths to holiness and spiritual wisdom, we find that other sides of the saints' personalities appear in these early stories. At times the saints seem to be living according to a different standard than that of the Sermon on the Mount. In some of the legends about Patrick, for example, we find him cursing his enemies, especially the druids, and in other ways attacking and punishing those who are opposed to him. Other monastic founders, voyagers, and missionaries sometimes employ similar means for maintaining their claims against each other or of vanquishing their foes. These stories reveal the influence of the earlier pagan culture and its own understanding of what constitutes a genuine hero.

According to the ancient Celts, their heroes, both male and female, were people of great physical beauty with unusual magical powers, including the ability to change shapes and even to transcend space and time. They also were flesh-and-blood individuals not only filled with human idealism but susceptible to human error. These heroes had strange visions, made voyages to other worlds, travelled in companies of friends, and endured great hardships for the tribe. Once the monks of the monasteries in 7th, 8th, and 9th centuries began to write down their remembrances of the early saints, they naturally presented them in a guise that the Celtic people would accept, and even expect of any of their heroes, including their religious ones. Thus, certain saints are portrayed as having virtues that one might associate with any warrior, such as strength, loyalty, and bravery. Practices too such as boasting and cursing were included in their descriptions of what the saints said and did.

The language of folktales, fairytales and dreams

Since the early hagiographers saw little demarcation between ordinary tales and religious ones, they often a blended the two. Frequently hagiographers incorporated into the Lives of the saints certain folktales which were popular at the time they wrote. Traces of these folktales appear in the stories of Brendan's voyage to the Promised Land; Brigit's talented fox at the court of an Irish king; David's marvellous horse which Findbarr rode across the Irish Sea; and Kevin's encounter with a fairy-witch.

Celtic hagiography is full of mythic components, the language of folktales, fairytales, and dreams. This language, related closely to the transforming power of symbols, was not used to deceive or to mislead readers of the hagiographies, but rather to provide them with intimations of the saint's greatness and assurances that each saint was especially loved, protected, and guided by God. Certain symbols and sacred numbers were used in the stories to enhance the saint's heroic reputation. The following are the most significant symbols to watch for as one reads the stories and sayings of the saints.

ANIMALS AND BIRDS

Joseph Campbell says that early tribes, living so close to nature, highly respected and revered animals and birds as 'tutors of humanity.' They were identified with specific qualities, and adopted as tribal totems and personal mentors. They symbolize our intuitive powers and helping instincts; to befriend them or to allow them to befriend us is to be guided by those powers and instincts. Among the ancient Celts, both wild and domestic animals were relied upon for food, clothing, transportation, and warmth. Animals of the hunt such as stags, boars, and bears are frequently depicted in art, while hunting itself was a ritual activity in which tribes called upon certain animals for their protection. Celtic literature is filled with references to birds, which were understood to be intermediaries between this world and the otherworld. Certain birds such as the owl and the dove were considered to have oracular abilities and prophetic powers. (This is clear in one of the stories of Brendan who is guided on his voyage by a bird who speaks to him.) The Celts were aware of the important contribution to human life of nature's creatures, and this conviction is behind the many references to animals and birds in the Lives of the Celtic saints. The more common animals and birds, along with their symbolic meaning, are the following:

Bee: A primary symbol of wisdom, bees were known for their industry in producing honey, one of the foods of the Promised Land. They were believed to be special creatures who took an acute interest in the affairs of their owners. If a bee entered a house it was considered a good omen. In his hagiography of Ninian of Whithorn, Aelred of Rievaulx compares that saint to a bee: 'Like a bee he formed for himself the honeycombs of wisdom.' Before the birth of David of Wales a symbol of his future wisdom, a honeycomb, appears to his father.

Boar: A symbol of strength and power, the boar was adopted by the Celts as an image of war because of its ferocity. It is found on surviving warrior helmets and armour. The boar also symbolized prosperity, because pork was a favourite Celtic food and played an important part in feasting. In a story of St. Kevin, he protects a wild boar, thus showing his respect for all of creation and perhaps of the wildest elements in himself.

Animals and birds as tutors of humanity

Cow: Because of the necessity of milk for sustenance and nourishment in early agricultural societies, a cow was considered to have quasi-mystical powers. Among Celts, it had great social value. There are numerous references in early and medieval literature concerning wars and cattle-raids. In the stories of the saints, Brigit's mother is a milkmaid and her newborn child is washed in milk, symbolizing Brigit's special character. Ciaran takes a white cow with him to Clonard. Her hide has miraculous powers, representing Ciaran's own intimacy with God. Samthann is said to never have had more than six cows, a reference to her conscious decision to remain poor.

Crane: In cultures ranging from the Chinese to those of the Mediterranean, the crane is a symbol of justice, longevity, and diligence. In Irish sagas, cranes represent women, and, because of their association with water, transformation as well. It is significant that Columcille was called 'the crane-cleric,' and that in a story about him he welcomes a poor crane with tenderness and kindness to Iona, possibly representing his love for his own feminine side.

Dove: A bird identified with the ability to speak of future happenings and act as a guide to the spiritual realm, the dove represented inspiration and spirituality for many early peoples. In Christianity, of course, it is a symbol of the Holy Spirit. Hagiographers, such as those of Brigit, Columcille, and David, used the dove in their stories to show how truly inspired and holy their saints were, with talents in preaching and teaching.

Fox: The fox is a popular character in many

indigenous stories, a symbol of cleverness and ingenuity. It even has shape-shifting abilities – as is true of Inari, the Japanese fox-deity. In Celtic folktales, the fox, compared to other animals, is the most frequent character that appears in them. It was often depicted as having the ability to outsmart other animals, although not always those which were domestic, such as the cat. Foxes appear in the earliest hagiographies, including those of Patrick and Brigit.

Horse: The horse, a symbol of fertility, sanctity, strength, speed, and sexual vigour, appears on many ancient Celtic coins. Horses were and are revered by the Celts, and were crucial to the Celtic way of life in a warrior society. Horses were especially associated with prestige and nobility. For Aidan of Lindisfarne to give his horse away was an important symbolic act of renunciation and humility; for Columcille to be mourned by a horse represented his own noble and saintly character.

Otter: A creature at home in two elements, land and water, the otter symbolized the union of the spiritual and natural realms. In Irish folklore otters were associated with omniscience, for Celts believed that otters slept with their eyes open, and thus did not miss anything, It is significant that Kevin, the Irish saint, and Cuthbert, the Northumbrian saint, both have friendly otters as helpmates.

Salmon: The salmon, a symbol of wisdom, is found in both Celtic sagas and saints' lives. According to the story of the hero Fionn Mac Cumhaill, nine magic hazel trees, containing all of the world's wisdom, grew on the banks of the pool of Fec, at the source of the river Boyne. The salmon of the pool, feeding on the nuts, stored that wisdom in themselves. By eating one of those fish Fionn acquired his magical knowledge of the otherworld. Among the stories of Brendan, we find the saint discovering salmon in the Land of Promise. In the account of Kevin, his community is threatened when one of the monks tries to kill the otter that brings salmon to it each night.

Stag: For hunters, the stag with its tree-like antlers symbolized the spirit of the forest, fertility, and virility. Because of the autumn shedding and spring growth of its antlers, reflecting the falling and reappearance of leaves on trees, the stag was also associated with seasonal changes. Among Celts, one of the most popular gods was Cernunnos, the horned one, who was depicted in human form with antlers on his head and a Celtic torc (bracelet) on each arm. Taking into account the stag's attributes, it is interesting to note that Patrick, in order to save himself and his men, changes them all into deer. In the story of David, the stag represents the child's future greatness and his conquest of good over evil.

Wolf: A sacred totem of many clans in Europe during early medieval times, the wolf symbolized the virtues of bravery and strength as well as the principle of evil (a werewolf). Wolves figure prominently in the biographies of pagan heroes, including the reputed founders of Rome, Remus and Romulus, who were said to have been suckled by a she-wolf. Because wolves burrow in the earth, Native Americans associate them with secret wisdom and spiritual power. The stories of Maedoc of Ferns are filled with references to wolves.

BREAD

Bread, a symbol of transformation and of unity, is produced by a process in which the original ingredients are changed significantly through baking, that is, being near the heat of a fire, another agent of transformation. Many ancient people, including the Jews, believed that sharing a meal gave spiritual life to the participants and was a sign of their common unity. Jesus followed in that tradition, making the Eucharist **the** act in which his followers would remember him while reminding themselves of their own brother and sisterhood. That ritual, originally celebrated in the homes of the early Christians, eventually was defined in belief and practice as one of the major sacraments of reconciliation of the Church. There are many references to the sharing of bread and of Eucharist in the hagiographies of the Celtic saints, including the story of Brendan and his fellow pilgrims celebrating Eucharist at certain sites each year, and another concerning Ciaran's fabulous bread which, like the Eucharist, had the ability to heal every sick person who ate of it.

FIRE

Fire is one of the most common symbols in the history of Judeo-Christian spirituality. It represents the power and presence of God. Images of fire, along with those of light, appear repeatedly in the writings of Christian wisdom figures from both the West and East. In the Scriptures, God speaks to Moses through a burning bush on Mount Sinai and tongues of fire are present at Pentecost. In the fourth century, the Egyptian desert mother, Amma Syncletica, describes God as a consuming fire, and John Cassian associates fire with the highest form of contemplative prayer; in the 12th century, Rhineland mystic Hildegard of Bingen relates how tongues of fire were with her during her spiritual awakening at midlife; and in the 14th century, English mystic, Richard Rolle, describes Jesus as a 'honeyed flame.' References to fire appear frequently in the stories of the Celtic saints. It is seen by neighbours at the house where Brigit sleeps as a child; it surrounds the room of Ita; and it ascends from the mouth of the holy virgin Samthann to the roof of her home. Bishop Erc sees Brendan's birthplace ablaze, and Ciaran is called 'a lamp, blazing with the light of wisdom.' Canair sees towers of fire rising from the churches of Ireland; Kevin carries fiery coals; Patrick lights the sacred fires on the Hill of Slane and his guardian angel speaks to him in a burning bush. All of these images and symbols are used by the hagiographers to say that these people were especially touched by God and manifestations of God's love.

HAIR

For many primitive peoples and by all sorts of religious traditions hair represents sexual energy, fertility, creativity, and vital strengths. Hair on one's head was a symbol of spiritual forces, intuitions, insights, spirituality, soul-power. Different colours of hair had specific connotations: brown or black hair symbolized dark, terrestrial energy, while golden hair was related to the sun's rays and represented intimacy with God. The length of one's hair and how it was worn also had significance. Samson's story in the Old Testament (Judges 16) tells how the hero was shorn of his strength and freedom when his hair was cut. In the early medieval church, as the priesthood evolved, two styles of tonsure came to symbolize two different ecclesial traditions. The 'Petrine' style in which a round spot towards the back of the head was shaved was a visible sign of one's dedication to Rome. The 'Celtic' style, probably a carry-over from the pagan druids, in which the whole of the front of the head from ear to ear was shaved while the hair behind was allowed to grow long represented

Representing the power and presence of God

devotion to Celtic spiritual traditions. Because of the symbolic importance of hair, these two different styles of tonsure became one of the major controversies dividing Roman and Celtic factions at the Synod of Whitby in 664. There are other references to hair that appear in the saints' Lives: Findbarr has fine hair, symbolizing his closeness to God, and is tonsured early in his life, signifying his vocation to priesthood; and, in the story of Ethne and Fedelm, the druid Caplit is converted and his hair cut to show his new loyalty to Christ, St. Patrick, and Rome.

OBJECTS

Certain objects frequently appear in the hagiographies of the Celtic saints that are especially equated with spiritual and therefore miraculous powers: a saint's bell, vestments, illuminated gospels (which remain dry in a rainstorm or when thrown into water!), crozier (a symbol of episcopal powers), or the stone or rock on which the saint or angel left imprints from hands, head, or feet. These were venerated by later generations as relics. To show the origins of these relics which were on display at the monasteries where pilgrims came, hagiographers included them in their accounts of the saints.

When these relics (such as books or bells) or

other objects (such as land or corn) are exchanged between the saints or given to each other's monasteries, they symbolize the love and mutuality between soulfriends, their equality and spiritual kinship. There are numerous references to this practice in the stories of the Celtic saints. The story of Brigit giving her father's sword away to a leper, however, has its own significance. In Celtic warrior society, the sword was a symbol of potency and virility; for Brigit to give it away symbolized that the source of her spiritual power was not in aggressiveness and intimidation but in mercy and compassion.

OIL

Oil has long been a symbol of healing, of inner strength, and of a life specially consecrated to God. The use of special oils for liturgical functions such as the consecration of kings and priests is a common occurrence in the Hebrew Scriptures. The practice was taken over by the Early Church and eventually used in the celebration of baptism, confirmation, and holy orders, as well as the consecration of churches and altars. In the hagiographies of the Celtic saints, oil is associated with certain saints. References to oil are found particularly in Findbarr's stories, including the vivid account of how oil flowed so abundantly at

Healing, fertility, wisdom, cleansing and rebirth

Cork where Findbarr built his church. This indicates that the church and Findbarr himself were sources of healing and spiritual strength.

TREES

Another common symbol, a tree denotes fertility, immortality, and wisdom; it can also connote one's roots and spiritual heritage. Mircea Eliade, a scholar of world religions, says a tree symbolizes absolute reality, the centre out of which all life flows, the life of the cosmos. The Hebrew Scriptures begin with the account of trees growing in the Garden of Eden: a 'Tree of Life' and a 'Tree of the Knowledge of Good and Evil' (Genesis 2:9). In the Book of Revelation, the last book of the Christian Scriptures, 'trees of life' are pictured near 'the river of life' in the heavenly Jerusalem (Revelation 22:2). Certain trees such as the beech and holly were revered by the ancient Celts. The oak tree especially was a symbol of wisdom, and the holly, a symbol of death and regeneration. Their spiritual leaders, the druids and druidesses, are said to have conducted their worship services and taught their students among sacred groves of oaks. A Celtic goddess of the grove, Nemetona, was worshipped at Bath in Britain and in Gaul. Tribal names also indicate close kinship between Celtic people and trees. In the stories of the saints, Samthann encounters a huge oak tree which she tames with her crozier, and, as we have seen, Ciaran and Enda share a vision of a tree growing in the centre of Ireland. The latter is similar to the vision which the Native American shaman, Black Elk, had as a child (and, like Julian of Norwich, while he was ill) which he believed contained regenerative powers for his tribe. Annie Dillard's description in *Pilgrim at Tinker Creek* of 'the tree with the lights in it' came to symbolize her own illumination and spiritual awakening. Among Christians, the Tree of Life found in Genesis becomes the cross on which Christ died, a symbol of God's love and of the way suffering can lead to reconciliation and the birth of compassion, a new way of relating to others and to oneself.

depths. Immersing oneself brought special stamina as well as control over one's anger and lust. The Celtic saints, as their stories show, are often found praying at night in lakes or oceans. Specific references to the regenerative powers of water appear in the story of a spring gushing forth at David's baptism; in the account of how a dead queen was raised to life by the water Findbarr had blessed; in the portrayal of Ita, on her death-bed, blessing water to heal Abbot Aengus; in the stream of water that gushed forth when Petroc, to impress his pagan sceptics, struck a rock with his staff. Christians through the ages have seen water as a special symbol of their own baptismal regeneration and rebirth through Christ.

WATER

Among many peoples and religious traditions water is a symbol of healing, cleansing, rebirth, and transformation. Because it can reflect light, it also is equated with luminosity and illumination. Water appears in the opening lines of the Book of Genesis and its account of creation; it is associated with Jesus's baptism and the beginning of his public ministry. In all its forms, from sacred springs to holy wells, water was venerated in the Celtic world. The ancient Celts believed that such places were the haunts of female deities. Special favours could be obtained, they thought, when offerings were thrown into the watery

SPECIAL NUMBERS

Besides the presence of these symbols in many of the stories of the Celtic saints, there are sacred numbers which had a meaning of their own. For ancient and medieval people, including Greeks, Romans, Jews, Gnostics, Kabbalists, and Celts (both ancient and Christian), certain numbers had special importance, because they believed that everything in this world was a reflection of a greater reality. Numbers, for them, expressed a divine order of things, invisible spiritual forces at work in the universe, a way of expressing and comprehending the meaning of existence. As such, numbers had mystical significance and were equated with spiritual power. Celtic hagiographers knew the symbolic value of these numbers. They used them in their texts to make theological points about the saint, and to increase the reputation and enhance the interest of their own storytelling. Each number had a particular character and meaning of its own. The numbers which appear most frequently in the stories of the Celtic saints are these:

Numbers had mystical significance and equated with spiritual power

Three: Three was a favourite number of Celtic folklore and hagiography. It was considered a powerful symbol of spiritual strength and intimacy with God, and it represented spiritual synthesis, the reconciliation of apparent opposites. Triads and triplisms had a remarkable fascination for the Celts, and both ancient and Christian Celts associated it with their deities. The ancient Celts expressed their belief that certain goddesses existed in groups of threes by representing them artistically in such reliefs as those of the 'Three Mothers' which appear in practically all parts of the Celtic world. Triplism was also manifest in the *tricephalos* (three-faced head) which is found on numerous vases or stones. Christian Celts symbolized their understanding of divinity with such symbols as the triangle or, as we find in legends about St. Patrick, the shamrock. In the stories of the Celtic saints, there are literally hundreds of references to threes – from the three angels who appear at Brigit's baptism to the three gifts God gives

to Columcille; from the three clerics who foster Findbarr to the three precious stones which appear in Ita's dreams. Even the greatest Celtic religious heroes, Patrick, Brigit, and Columcille, are referred to in common parlance today as 'the holy trinity of Irish saints.'

Four: This number symbolized wholeness and harmonious completion. The medieval mind associated the number four with the earth, the four directions of the world, and the seasons. Celts subdivided their land into four quarters, and, according to the lawbooks in northern Wales, there were four acres in a homestead. On the Isle of Man, four quarterlands at one time formed a *treen*, the smallest unit for administrative purposes. References to the number four appear in the stories of Ciaran with his four sacks of consecrated wheat, of Brigit who cures four sick persons at a certain church, and of Ita who requests four acres of land on which to live.

Five: Another symbol of wholeness, the number five appears in a large number of secular and religious texts. In the Middle Ages it was primarily associated with the Virgin Mary, and was generally seen as the number signifying True Faith. Medieval Ireland had five great roads and five celebrated hostels; in its literature, mythical persons wear fivefold cloaks, and the greatest

Irish hero, Cu Chulainn, has five wheels carved on his shield which in the ancient world represented the cosmos. In the stories of the saints, Hild has five students who become bishops, Brendan is fostered by Ita for five years, and Patrick has five companions with him at Tara when he confronts the pagan king.

Seven: A mystical number of special importance for ancient peoples, including Greeks, Romans, Jews, and Celts, it symbolized perfection, perfect order, a complete period or cycle, harmony. Seven is as popular as the number nine in some branches of Celtic literature, and of course appears in the saints' stories: Brendan sails for seven years before he reaches the elusive Land of Promise; Cuthbert's spiritual mentor, Boisil, dies on the seventh day; Hild endures a painful illness for seven years; an angel comes to Patrick on the seventh day of each week; Kevin lives for seven years in the wilderness.

Disclosing 'inner' realities: visionary experiences, intuitions and dreams

Nine: Another prominent mystical number in Celtic tradition which was important in divinations and folk cures, nine symbolized great spiritual power, health, fulfilment. Dante was later to equate the number nine with Beatrice whom he loved dearly and who acts as his guide to heaven in his *Divine Comedy*. In Irish literature, there are repeated allusions to companies of nine, which consist of a leader with eight followers,

and to houses comprising nine rooms. In Wales there also was a tradition that a complete house should consist of nine component parts. An early Welsh poem mentions the breath of nine maidens which kindles a certain magical fountain, while in an Irish tale the hero Ruad swims to a secret place and finds nine fair women with whom he sleeps for nine nights under the sea on nine beds of bronze. Nine was evidently a significant unit of time for the Celts, for some scholars assert that they had a nine-day week, or rather a nine-night week, since they reckoned by nights, not days. In the stories of the saints, the number nine or its variant appears quite often: Kevin dies at the age of 129, nine heavenly orders of angels are mentioned in the account of Findbarr's death, Non naturally prepares for the birth of David at the end of her ninth month of pregnancy, and a famous Irish high-king is called Niall of the Nine Hostages.

Twelve: An ancient symbol signifying wholeness or completeness, the number twelve has special meaning, for it is found in many spiritual traditions. In Greek mythology, Odysseus has twelve companions; in the Hebrew Scriptures, there are twelve tribes of Israel; in the Christian gospels twelve apostles accompany Jesus; and, in later medieval legends, King Arthur has twelve knights of the Round Table. We today celebrate twelve months of the year. The Celtic hagiographers respected this number's spiritual significance too by using it often in their portrayal of the saints: Aidan lives twelve days after the death of the king he loved; Finnian educates the 'Twelve Apostles of Ireland'; Findbarr builds twelve churches and is accompanied to Rome by twelve monks; David founds twelve monasteries. Kevin's hagiographer, evidently in order to outdo Brigit's, has twelve angels at Kevin's baptism rather than only three!

We need not be surprised by the symbols and sacred numbers which are found in the early stories and sayings of the saints, for throughout human history this symbolic language was used by people not only to describe mysterious events in the 'outer world' which can be perceived by the human eye (if not always understood!), but also to disclose 'inner' realities: visionary experiences, feelings, intuitions, dreams. These inner experiences, of course, are no less real than the outer ones, for they often determine and profoundly influence the shape and course of outer events, as well as the development of character: the distinctive qualities or traits emerging from our deeper selves, what the ancients called, quite simply, our souls. All primitive peoples, including the writers of the gospels, the fathers and mothers of the early church, and the Christian Celts, did not invent the great mysteries which are described in the saints' lives, such as birth, love, suffering, forgiveness, death,

and rebirth. They **experienced** them first. If we can identify with them at that level of awareness, we can begin to see that the stories of the Celtic saints, female and male, are really stories about ourselves. They are about our own ability (with the help of God and others, of course) to transcend human pain and suffering, and, in the process, experience various forms of transformation. Sometimes we undergo such a profound change of heart that it seems we will never be the same again.

Listening with the heart

By now it should be clear that we need to approach the stories and sayings of the Celtic saints with less of a critical eye to whether events in this or that saint's life are historically accurate or verifiable, but rather, as earlier generations did, with an openness to what the stories themselves might teach us about God, holiness, and our own great mysteries. Such an approach presumes that some understanding of the Early Celtic Church's history and spirituality, as well as the significance of symbols and sacred numbers which appear in hagiographies, can help us appreciate their content. It also presupposes that while the stories of the saints contain explicit messages about Christian spirituality and what it means to be fully human today there is more to these texts than the eye can see or the mind take in. To grasp fully and begin to integrate their spiritual wisdom, we must bring a willingness to reflect quietly upon them, and to discern unhurriedly their sometimes hidden meaning. What we especially need to bring to these stories and sayings is a compassionate, attentive, listening heart.

By quietly listening to the description of the stages, transitions, and miraculous deeds of a saint's life, we can begin to discern and appreciate our life patterns as well as our own kinship with Jesus. We also might start to recall the happenings (sometimes wondrous?!) told about our birth and early years, and to remember gratefully who our significant mentors were and how they touched our lives. As we read the stories, we might consider what sort of leadership we are presently offering others and what gifts of ours might make a great difference ('miraculous'?) in their lives. In our prayerful reflection, we might identify what sorts of trials and tribulations we have encountered, and what we have learned in our own 'school of suffering.' We might ask ourselves what journeys we have already bravely embarked upon – and, if we are to be true to ourselves, what new explorations we may yet have to undertake. We might also, in our quieter moments of listening to the heart, acknowledge with love those

Knowledge of self, compassion for others and friendship with God

special people who have died, and what legacy they have passed on to us about the sacredness of life and awesomeness of dying.

By bringing both heart and mind to the stories of the Celtic saints – and to our own life experiences – we will truly discover and make our own their wisdom, a wisdom that is much more than a mere accumulation of historical knowledge and facts. It is, rather, a way of life, a spirituality lived gratefully each day, one day at a time.

To read the stories and sayings of the saints and to listen to them with the heart is to rediscover the wisdom which the early church already knew: that being a saint is the vocation to which we all are called, not just the 'greats' who lived long ago or those whom the church now officially canonizes or beatifies. Being a saint is simply centring our lives in God's, and, through our work and ministries, helping others discover perhaps the hardest thing of all: that God's compassion and forgiveness embrace everyone.

To reflect prayerfully on the lives of the early Celtic saints reveals that wisdom is nothing more – and nothing less – than knowledge of self, compassion for others, and friendship with God. If we cultivate those qualities and relationships in our lives, Christ and the saints will truly live in us, as we live in them.

For the wisdom of those saints is still very much alive. Like the tiny coracle boats of the Celtic missionaries skimming swiftly over the ocean depths, they travel on in our dreams and our imagination. They give us a rich vision of a more inclusive church, and perhaps new directions in our own spirituality. They teach us the importance of friendship, and how it is a vehicle to God. They challenge us to be attentive to and more trusting of the gentle, yet ever persistent call of God in our human experiences and in our hearts.

By turning to the stories of the Celtic saints, we can allow them to become guides to the spiritual heritage which is ours and to the best which lies within us. As friends and mentors of our souls, they can help us become more conscious and appreciative of the ancient spiritual traditions in which we stand, so that we might begin to pray not only with our lips and our intellects, but out of the very roots of our lives. Most of all, they show us wisdom, a Christian wisdom that continues to flourish, like Ciaran's tree growing in the middle of Ireland, capable of teaching all sorts of people, including those who live far across the Irish Sea.

©2006 Edward C. Sellner

Books by Edward C. Sellner

Wisdom of the Celtic Saints: Revised and Expanded Edition
St. Paul, MN: Bog Walk Press, 2006

Mentoring: the Ministry of Spiritual Kinship
Cambridge, MA: Cowley Press, 2002

Pilgrimage: Exploring a Great Spiritual Practice
Notre Dame, IN: Sorin Books, 2004

The Celtic Soul Friend
Notre Dame, IN: Ave Maria Press, 2002

Stories of the Celtic Soul Friends: Their Meaning for Today
New York: Paulist Press, 2004